the
UNIVERSE

→ YOU

YOU

the

UNIVERSE

nothing
is missing.

you are
already
whole.

Made out of Stars

A JOURNAL for SELF-REALIZATION

Meera Lee Patel

PARTICULAR BOOKS
an imprint of
PENGUIN BOOKS

PARTICULAR BOOKS

UK | USA | Canada | Ireland | Australia
India | New Zealand | South Africa

Particular Books is part of the Penguin Random House group of companies
whose addresses can be found at global.penguinrandomhouse.com

First published in the USA by TarcherPerigee 2018
First published in Great Britain by Particular Books 2018
004

Copyright © Meera Lee Patel, 2018

The moral right of the author has been asserted

Book design by Meera Lee Patel
Author photograph by Lindsay Grace Whiddon

Printed and bound in Italy by Printer Trento

A CIP catalogue record for this book is available from the British Library

ISBN: 978-0-241-35526-8

www.greenpenguin.co.uk

To you, for being who you are.

This world wouldn't be what it is without you.

INTRODUCTION

✳ ✳ ✳

These days, it's all too easy to feel disconnected and overwhelmed. Phone calls and tight deadlines take priority over fresh air and honest conversations, and it's not always easy to pull meaning from the little things that take up so much of our time. Self-care is usually the last item on a very long to-do list that grows longer and longer each day—and yet it's essential. If we can't find love for ourselves, how can we love anything or anyone else?

The stars we see shining above us are far away, but they still rise with us in the early morning. When nightfall shrouds us with its heavy cloak, they glitter and remind us that there is light in the darkest of places. Stars are composed of various elements—carbon, hydrogen, nitrogen, oxygen, sulfur, and phosphorus—and are held together by their own gravity.

Like stars, we are each held together by our own indescribable forces: tiny beacons of light that glow within us, making us who we are—one-of-a-kind beings privy to a spectrum of emotion, ambitions, and dreams. When you realize this, it becomes impossible to wish you were anyone else. In a world that continually tells you to change who you are, it becomes much easier to be honest and intentional—to be exactly as you are.

Know this: The very things that create glittering, ethereal stars are inside you. There is star-stuff in your hands, your eyes, your heart. The light that glows inside us, making us who we are, also connects us to each other and everything else in the world.

If you can make an effort to remember this, the little not-so-fun things become much more manageable—and oftentimes they become sources of meaning in difficult moments. There can be purpose in every small step we take, no matter how insignificant it seems at the time. There is purpose in the smallest acts of kindness, brief encounters with a stranger, the quiet moments in which you extend grace to yourself.

Feeling connected to the world begins by nurturing the connection you have with yourself. As you continue to know and understand yourself more clearly, you'll recognize a tiny piece of yourself everywhere—in the plants, animals, and people around you, and on the darkest of nights, even in the stars.

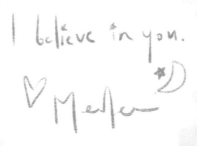

I'M
NOT AFRAID
OF STORMS,
FOR I'M LEARNING
HOW TO SAIL MY SHIP.

LOUISA MAY ALCOTT

The more we learn about ourselves, the easier it becomes to navigate obstacles we face.

What are you learning about yourself now?

What did you learn about yourself a year ago?

What do you hope to learn about yourself a year from now?

When we don't make the time to take care of ourselves, it becomes impossible for our bodies, minds, and hearts to remain in harmony.

Write about how you take care of yourself now.

How do you hope to take care of yourself
a year from now?

LIVE!
LIVE THE WONDERFUL LIFE
THAT IS IN YOU! LET NOTHING
BE LOST UPON YOU.
BE ALWAYS
SEARCHING FOR NEW
SENSATIONS.

BE AFRAID of NOTHING.

OSCAR WILDE

When was the last time you experienced something new?

What are three things
you've always wanted to experience?

What is keeping you from exploring them?

Remember, this—THAT VERY LITTLE IS NEEDED TO MAKE A happy life.

MARCUS AURELIUS

Write about three fulfilling aspects of your life
that you tend to overlook.

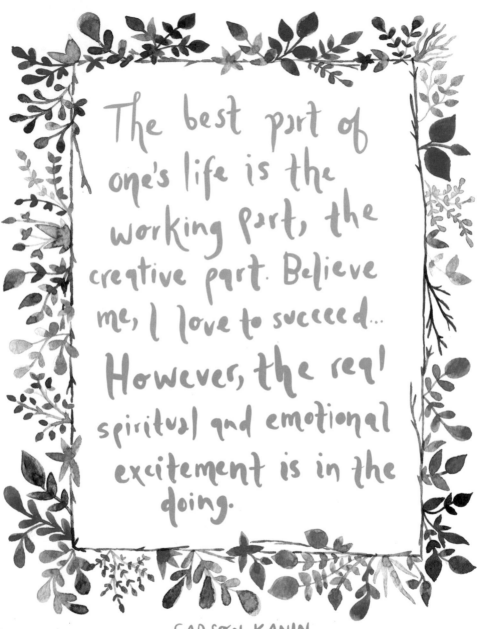

The best part of one's life is the working part, the creative part. Believe me, I love to succeed... However, the real spiritual and emotional excitement is in the doing.

GARSON KANIN

Think of something you dread doing on a daily basis.
Can you take more pride in the simple act of doing?

EVERYTHING IS MADE OUT
OF *magic*, LEAVES AND TREES,
FLOWERS AND BIRDS, BADGERS AND
FOXES AND SQUIRRELS AND
PEOPLE. SO IT MUST
BE ALL AROUND US.

FRANCES
HODGSON BURNETT

Feeling connected to the world means observing it closely. Notice nature: how you carry a part of it with you wherever you go. Take a walk in the woods and practice feeling at home in the great outdoors.

Write about this experience here.

WHAT MAKES YOU FEEL CONNECTED TO . . .
your heart, your spirit, your sense of self?

THE MOMENT YOU DOUBT
WHETHER YOU CAN FLY,
YOU CEASE FOREVER TO
BE ABLE TO DO IT...

TO HAVE FAITH IS TO
HAVE WINGS.

J.M. BARRIE

Think of something you've felt unsure about for a long time. What would help you have more faith in yourself?

It's no use
going back to yesterday,
because I WAS A
DIFFERENT
PERSON then.

LEWIS CARROLL

Each one of us is constantly evolving.
How have you changed for the better in the past year?

I MUST BE TAKEN AS I HAVE BEEN MADE. The SUCCESS is not mine, the FAILURE is not mine, BUT THE TWO TOGETHER MAKE ME.

CHARLES DICKENS

Describe an achievement or a failure you have been defining yourself by. Is it possible that who you are exists outside of your successes and failures?

The world is like
A GREAT MIRROR,
and reflects our lives
JUST AS WE OURSELVES
look upon it.

L. FRANK
BAUM

Sometimes the best thing we can do to change our
lives is change our perspective of it.

List ten ways you are living a lucky life.

1.

2.

3.

4.

5.

6.

7.

8.

9.

10.

WHAT MAKES YOU FEEL CONNECTED TO . . .
your body and breath?

Adopt
the pace of
nature; her
secret is
patience.

RALPH WALDO EMERSON

What are three things you are impatient with in your life? How can you practice patience with each one?

What more can the world offer you than countless BREATHS to hold in your lungs and countless HOURS to do with what you WISH?

The world offers us so much.
Write about the possibilities you have in life.

My enemy said to me,
"LOVE YOUR
ENEMY,"
And I obeyed
him and
LOVED
MYSELF.

KHALIL GIBRAN

When was the last time you felt self-critical?
How can you love yourself better in these moments?

This
is the greatest
work that
kindness
does to others,
that it makes
them kind
themselves.

Frederick William Faber

What was the last kind thing someone did for you?
How did it make you more kind?

WHAT MAKES YOU FEEL
CONNECTED TO . . . a stranger?

WHAT MAKES YOU FEEL CONNECTED
TO . . . yourself?

The greatest deception men suffer is from their own opinions.

LEONARDO da VINCI

We are often self-critical, to our own detriment.

Identify three traits in yourself that you have trouble accepting. What is one positive aspect of each trait?

1. Trait:
   Positive aspect:

2. Trait:
   Positive aspect:

3. Trait:
   Positive aspect:

PERHAPS
EVERYTHING
THAT FRIGHTENS
US IS, IN ITS
DEEPEST ESSENCE,
SOMETHING
HELPLESS THAT
WANTS OUR
LOVE.

RAINER MARIA RILKE

List three things that scare you.
How can you offer love to each one?

1. Fear:
   Action:

2. Fear:
   Action:

3. Fear:
   Action:

Think of all the beauty
in yourself and in everything
around you and be happy.
ANNE FRANK

Describe three beautiful things about:

YOU

YOUR HOME

YOUR COUNTRY

YOUR PLANET

YOUR UNIVERSE

FREEDOM IS LOVING YOURSELF.

List five ways you can be kinder to yourself.

IF YOU
BREATHE
IN AND ARE
AWARE that
YOU ARE ALIVE—

THAT YOU CAN
TOUCH THE
MIRACLE
OF BEING ALIVE—
THEN THAT IS
A kind of
ENLIGHTENMENT.

THICH NAHT HAHN

Breathe in. Recognize that you are alive in a world that is very much alive. What does it mean to be alive?

YOUR TASK IS *NOT* TO SEEK FOR LOVE,
BUT MERELY TO SEEK AND FIND ALL THE
BARRIERS WITHIN YOURSELF THAT
YOU HAVE BUILT AGAINST IT.

HELEN SHUCMAN

What are the obstacles keeping love and positivity out
of your life? How can you dissolve them?

WHAT MAKES YOU FEEL CONNECTED TO . . .
the human race?

LIFE IS NOT EASY for any of us. But what of that? WE MUST HAVE PERSEVERANCE AND ABOVE ALL CONFIDENCE IN OUR SELVES. WE must BELIEVE that WE ARE GIFTED FOR SOMETHING.

MARIE CURIE

Write about three gifts you have to offer the world.

1.

2.

3.

NO ONE IS USELESS IN THIS WORLD WHO LIGHTENS THE BURDEN OF IT FOR ANYONE ELSE.

Charles Dickens

How does it feel to help someone close to you?
Can you cultivate that same feeling by
helping a stranger?

I CAN SO
CLEARLY DISTINGUISH
BETWEEN THE CRIMINAL
AND HIS CRIME;

I CAN SO SINCERELY FORGIVE
THE FIRST WHILE I
ABHOR THE LAST.

CHARLOTTE BRONTË

Think of an action or statement that hurt you recently. What was the motivation behind it? How can you forgive the person who hurt you?

I felt in love, not with anything or anybody in particular but with everything.

GEORGE HARRISON

What is most beautiful about . . .

The morning light in your room?

The first tree you see today?

A stranger on the street?

The first piece of news you read?

Taking some time for yourself today?

The last conversation you had?

WHAT MAKES YOU FEEL CONNECTED TO . . .
someone you have a difficult relationship with?

I have always believed,
and I still believe,
that whatever
good or bad
fortune
may come our way
we can always give it
meaning and
transform it
into something else.

HERMANN HESSE

Describe your best and worst experiences over the past year. What did you learn from each experience?

BEING ALIVE
IS THE MAGIC—
BEING STRONG
IS THE MAGIC.
THE MAGIC
IS IN ME.
THE MAGIC
IS IN ME.

FRANCES HODGSON BURNETT

It's easy to look for magic in things outside ourselves, but it is something that exists within each of us. When was the last time you recognized all the possibility and wonder inside you? Write about it here.

THE PLANt
STRUGGLING UNDER A
STONE DOES NOT KNOW
ITS OWN CONDITION.
ONLY WHEN THE STONE
IS REMOVED CAN IT
SPRING UP FREELY INtO THE
LIGHt.

PEARL S. BUCK

What is one obstacle (a person, a feeling, a challenge) keeping you from being your true self?
How can you move past it?

I DO NOT THINK THE FOREST WOULD BE SO BRIGHT, NOR THE WATER SO WARM, NOR LOVE SO SWEET, IF THERE WERE NO DANGER IN THE LAKES.

C.S. LEWIS

Life is a balance. Reflect on a difficult time in your life. How did that period prepare you for something good that came later?

WE MAY ACT SOPHISTICATED
AND WORLDLY, BUT I BELIEVE WE
FEEL SAFEST WHEN WE GO
INSIDE OURSELVES AND FIND
HOME, A PLACE WHERE WE
BELONG AND MAYBE THE
ONLY PLACE WE REALLY
DO.

MAYA ANGELOU

What makes you feel safe within yourself?

WHERE ARE YOU NOW that YOU ASk
THIS QUESTION? ARE YOU IN the
WORLD OR IS the WORLD
WITHIN YOU?

RAMANA MAHARSHI

Close your eyes and imagine the universe is inside you,
the same way you are inside it.
Write about this feeling.

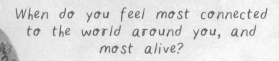
When do you feel most connected
to the world around you, and
most alive?

EACH
FRIEND
REPRESENTS

A WORLD
IN US, A

WORLD POSSIBLY
NOT BORN UNTIL
THEY ARRIVE, AND

IT IS
ONLY BY THIS
MEETING THAT

A NEW WORLD
IS BORN.

ANAÏS NIN

How many worlds have other people created inside you? Write about them here.

I AM A SHIPWRECKED MAN WHO FEARS EVERY SEA.

OVID

If you let your fears paralyze you, you'll never take a step forward. What is something you are currently afraid of? How can you move forward alongside that fear?

WHAT MAKES YOU FEEL CONNECTED TO . . .
the stars and universe?

There is
NOTHING
either
GOOD or BAD,
but THINKING
makes it so.

WILLIAM SHAKESPEARE

Reflect on an issue you've been struggling with recently.
Is it possible to see both sides of the story?
What can you learn from each side?

There
is BEAUTY in
the sorrow that
drapes itself over your
shoulders, THERE
IS BEAUTY in the pain
that shakes and stuns
your heart, and THERE IS
BEAUTY in having the
strength to start over,
AGAIN and AGAIN.

Think about a time of deep sadness in your life.
What beautiful things have come from this sorrow?
How have you changed because of it?

EVERY ONE IS A MOON,

AND HAS A DARK SIDE WHICH
HE NEVER SHOWS TO ANYBODY.

* MARK TWAIN *

Think about something that you're ashamed of.
Does the shame come from yourself or others? What
is one step you can take to reconcile
this shame within yourself?

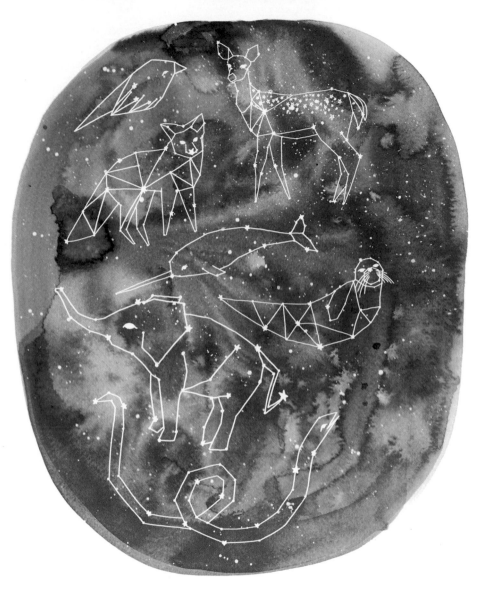

WE ARE ALL
connected

What makes you feel most connected to people you haven't met and places you haven't seen yet?

With freedom,
flowers, books, and the
moon, who could
not be perfectly
happy?

OSCAR WILDE

What are the four things you most need to be happy
from the list below?

SAFETY   CONTENTMENT   LOVE

            RESPECT   SELF-ACCEPTANCE

SUCCESS   FAMILY   AMBITION

        HEALTHY RELATIONSHIPS   HOME

SELF-RESPECT   MONEY

            GROWTH   KNOWLEDGE

Do you already have them?

Can any of them be found within you?

Reshape
yourself through
the power of
your will;
never let
yourself be
degraded
by self-will.

KRISHNA

Holding on to regrets and criticizing ourselves for our mistakes are how we keep from becoming better, kinder people to ourselves and others.

What is one thing you can do to reshape yourself in a loving, noncritical way?

I celebrate myself,
and sing myself,

And what I assume you
shall assume,

For every atom belonging
to me as good belongs to you.

WALT WHITMAN

Five things I love and appreciate about myself:

1.

2.

3.

4.

5.

Five things I love and appreciate about someone else:

1.

2.

3.

4.

5.

WHAT MAKES YOU FEEL CONNECTED TO . . .
a person you care deeply about?

WHAT MAKES YOU FEEL CONNECTED TO . . .
a person you feel distant from?

a light
here
required
a
shadow
there.

VIRGINIA WOOLF

What are the darker traits within you?
What are the positive traits that balance them?

DARK:

POSITIVE:

DARK:

POSITIVE:

DARK:

POSITIVE:

DARK:

POSITIVE:

IMAGINATION IS MORE IMPORTANT THAN KNOWLEDGE.
FOR KNOWLEDGE IS LIMITED, WHEREAS IMAGINATION
EMBRACES THE ENTIRE WORLD.

ALBERT EINSTEIN

Imagine a better world for yourself and others.
What does it look and sound like?

SEEKING MEANS: having A GOAL.
BUT FINDING MEANS: being FREE,
BEING OPEN, HAVING
NO GOAL.

HERMANN HESSE

What is the biggest goal you have for yourself in the next year? If you resolve to be open to all possibilities, does that goal change?

Wisdom is the daughter of experience.

LEONARDO DA VINCI

What are five important lessons you've learned
in the past year?

The
peace you
are looking
for is inside
you.

When do you feel most at peace? What are three things you can do to find this peace internally?

EACH ONE OF US —
ANIMAL, PLANT, MAN,
AND STAR — IS A TINY FIBER
OF AN INTRICATELY WOVEN
WORK. EACH FIBER HOLDS A
UNIQUE BEAUTY THAT
CANNOT BE REPLICATED
OR REPLACED — AND
IF A SINGLE STITCH
GOES MISSING,
THE PICTURE
IS INCOMPLETE.

What is something you bring to this world
that no one else does?

you are connected to me;
i am connected to you;
we are made out of the
moons and stars
in the sky.

LET YOUR OWN
UNIVERSE GUIDE YOU

* * *

Find your own
mountain to climb.

your
path
won't look
like

anyone
else's,
and that's
OK

let the
vastness
of the
world fill
you up.

Find
the stars
inside
you.

Spend
time
building
a home
within
yourself

look for
the
stars in
others.

Close your
eyes and retreat
inward as
often as you
can.

Like everything else,
you have no beginning or
end.

Each day is another
chance to be exactly who
you are.

FURTHER READING

✱   ✱   ✱

Quotations appear from the following publications:

A Course in Miracles by Helen Schucman and William Thetford (Course in Miracles Society, 1976)

Alice's Adventures in Wonderland by Lewis Carroll (Macmillan, 1865)

The Beatles Anthology (Chronicle Books, 2000)

The Bhagavad Gita by Eknath Easwaran (Nilgiri Press, 2007)

The Complete Works by Ralph Waldo Emerson (Houghton, Mifflin, 1904)

The Core Teachings of Ramana Maharshi by Ramana Maharshi (LuLu Press, 2012)

The Diary of a Young Girl by Anne Frank (Bantam, 1993)

The Diary of Anaïs Nin, Vol. 2 by Anaïs Nin (The Swallow Press: Harcourt, Brace & World, 1967)

De Profundis: The Ballad of Reading Gaol and Other Writings by Oscar Wilde (Wordsworth Editions, 1999)

Following the Equator by Mark Twain (American Publishing Company, 1897)

Great Expectations by Charles Dickens (Chapman & Hall, 1861)

Hamlet by William Shakespeare

Jayne Eyre by Charlotte Brontë

Leaves of Grass by Walt Whitman (David McKay, 1892)

Letter to My Daughter by Maya Angelou (Random House Publishing Group, 2008)

Letters to a Young Poet by Rainer Maria Rilke (New World Library, 2010)

Little Women by Louisa May Alcott (Roberts Brothers, 1868)

The Little White Bird by J. M. Barrie (Hodder & Stoughton, 1902)

Living Buddha, Living Christ by Thich Naht Hahn (Riverhead Books, 1994)

Madame Curie: A Biography by Eve Curie Labouisse (Da Capo Press, 1937)

Meditations by Marcus Aurelius (Dover Publications, 1997)

Metamorphoses by Ovid (Oxford University Press, 2009)

The Notebooks of Leonardo da Vinci, XIX Philosophical Maxims. Morals.
    Polemics and Speculations, by Leonardo Da Vinci (Dover, 1970)

"On Kindness in General" (sermon) by Frederick William Faber, *Spiritual
    Conferences*, 1860.

Siddhartha by Hermann Hesse (New Directions Publishing, 1922)*Our Mutual
    Friend* by Charles Dickens (Chapman & Hall, 1865)

Out of the Silent Planet by C. S. Lewis (John Lane, 1938)

The Picture of Dorian Gray by Oscar Wilde (Lippincott's Monthly Magazine,
    1890)

Rinkitink in Oz by Frank L. Baum (Reilly & Britton, 1916)

The Secret Garden by Frances Hodgson Burnett (Frederick A. Stokes, 1911)

Self Reliance by Ralph Waldo Emerson (Roycrofters, 1908)

Spiritual Sayings of Kahlil Gibran by Kahlil Gibran (Citadel, 1965)

This I Believe (radio broadcast) with Pearl S. Buck, 1951.

To The Lighthouse by Virginia Woolf (Hogarth Press, 1927)

Wit and Wisdom by John. W. Gardner and Francesca Gardner Reese (W. W.
    Norton & Company, 1996)

"What Life Means to Einstein: An Interview by George Sylvester Viereck"
    originally printed in *The Saturday Evening Post*, October 1929.

NOTES

★ ★ ★

ACKNOWLEDGMENTS

Self-realization is the process of recognizing or unsheathing your true Self. It is an intimate practice and often requires solitude—but if you are lucky, as I have been, many will help you along your way.

I am grateful to my parents who first introduced me to the concept of self-realization, the perception that there are numerous worlds inside of me, and the belief that I have the ability to unify them.

I am grateful to the following people, who have helped me recognize the many worlds inside me: Ojus, Karishma, Kristen, Alicia, Amanda, and Trevor. You are my stars.
And I am grateful to Arian and Shea, who have each created another world inside of me.

Lastly, I am grateful to both Marian and Laurie, who help me share who I am with this vast, mysterious world we live in.

ABOUT THE AUTHOR

✦ ✦ ✦

Meera Lee Patel is a self-taught writer and artist who knows, for certain, that there are many worlds, many moons, and many stars inside of her. She likes sleeping and smiling and believes that all change comes from within.

She knows there are many worlds inside you, too, and she hopes you will look for them all.

To see more of her work, please visit MeeraLee.com.

To read her thoughts and see her smiles, please visit Instagram.com/meeraleepatel.

ALSO BY *Meera Lee Patel:*

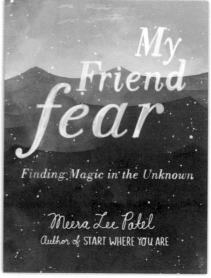

WWW.MEERALEE.COM/BOOKS